Read ☆ Draw ☆ Remember
American History
～ ACTIVITIES ～

by Jeff Lantos

NEW YORK • TORONTO • LONDON • AUCKLAND • SYDNEY
MEXICO CITY • NEW DELHI • HONG KONG • BUENOS AIRES

SCHOLASTIC
Teaching
Resources

Dedication

For my Mom and Dad with love

❋•°❋•°❋•°❋•°❋•°❋•°❋•°❋•°❋•°❋•°❋•°❋•❋

Acknowledgments

Many thanks to my student-artists who've contributed to this book. Over the years they've taken historical episodes and abstract concepts and turned them into the eye-catching, whimsical, and poignant works of art that you'll see in these pages. These artists are Ilana Arbisser, Audrey Ashraf, Danielle Beilinson, Maya Bendifallah, Jessica Bornstein, Julie Cron, Alison Eagle, Elliott Engelmann, Sasha Engelmann, Adam Estrin, Kendra Filler, Kristina Goldenberg, Jennifer Gurvis, Chloe Hamilton, Jordan Hart, Alex Hartenstein, Ji Won Hong, Grayson Ishimatsu, Lindsay Jacobs, Caroline Merz, Erin Newman, Rebecca Ouligian, Jade Robertson-Fusco, Kristina Roman, Sara Rosenthal, Jamie Samuel, Rose Schlaff, Stephanie Taft, Diana Yu, Hilary Yu, and Adrian Wieshofer. May you continue to integrate history and the graphic arts.

In writing the historical commentaries, I relied on a number of sources including Joy Hakim's lucid, honest, and witty series of textbooks, *The History of Us*, which we read every day in our class. I also dipped into *Undaunted Courage* by Stephen Ambrose, *Crucible of War* by Fred Anderson, *What's the Deal? Jefferson, Napolean and the Louisiana Purchase* by Rhoda Blumberg, *Miracle at Philadelphia* by Catherine Drinker Bowen, *The Adams-Jefferson Letters* edited by Lester J. Cappon, *The Columbia Encyclopedia*, fifth edition, edited by Barbara Chernow and George A. Vallasi, *The Spirit of Seventy-six* edited by Henry Steele Commager and Richard B. Morris, *Guns, Germs, and Steel* by Jared Diamond, *The Golden Threads* by Hannah Josephson, *The Name of War* by Jill Lepore, *American Railroads* by John Stover, *Ordeal by Hunger: The Story of the Donner Party* by George Stewart, *Paul Revere's Ride* by David Hackett Fischer, and *Lincoln* by David Herbert Donald.

❋•°❋•°❋•°❋•°❋•°❋•°❋•°❋•°❋•°❋•°❋•°❋•❋

Cover design by Gerard Fuchs

Interior design by Sydney Wright

ISBN 0-439-38519-9

Printed in the U.S.A.

1 2 3 4 5 6 7 8 9 10   40   09 08 07 06 05 04 03

Contents

Introduction

As a teacher, I am always looking for new and better ways to help students absorb information and retain it. In math, students solve problem after problem, day after day. In reading, they get pulled into a narrative because they identify or empathize with a character. In science, students memorize body parts and the table of the elements. But history is different. History does not come with any built-in reinforcement strategies. History is also full of abstract notions such as democracy, balance of power, and class conflict. So the challenge for a history teacher is to devise follow-up activities that engage students, illuminate lessons, and promote retention of the material.

I have found that art—or more specifically, cartooning—addresses all three concerns. Drawing history cartoons is a way to make the abstract concrete and a way to make past events more than names and dates on a time line. Not only that, it is teacher-friendly. All you need is paper, pencils, markers or crayons, and a sample cartoon.

In presenting the first cartoon assignment, an important concept to discuss with your students is the difference between the literal and the symbolic. Cartoons should not rely on actual illustrations of people or events. Rather students should utilize symbols such as trees, food, animals, and so forth, that represent people, countries, armies, documents, or institutions. This is a general discussion that you will probably need to have only once or twice. After that, students will get it.

To begin a particular assignment, I write on the board the proposed cartoon title. Then I distribute a photocopy of a sample cartoon. This sample—and the assignments in this book—should be regarded as suggestions. Encourage students to strike out on their own and to use creativity and humor. I am always surprised by how ingenious, original, whimsical, and sophisticated many of the cartoons are, especially after students have drawn a few. I allot at least 15 minutes of class time for brainstorming and discussion. If students have trouble coming up with ideas, I first give them general advice. Suppose the cartoon assignment is "England and France Fight for Land in America." I will say, "Think about two predators fighting over prey." If a student is still stuck, I will give specific advice. "How about two mice fighting over a piece of cheese?" Sometimes the student will use this idea. More often than not, my suggestion will lead students to their own concept. I have found

that once students have a concept that works, the cartoon can usually be completed in an hour.

I assign a cartoon every Monday and collect them on Friday. They can be used to cap a unit, to illuminate a theme or a big event, or to reinforce one of the standards. The cartoons themselves are also learning tools since they require students to fuse not only art and history, but also geography, statistics, writing, persuasion, and cause and effect. Some cartoons also call for higher level thinking skills such as comparing, contrasting, and synthesizing.

In assessing the work, I first look for a title and check to see that the symbols are correctly labeled (a tree is seldom just a tree). Dates must be included whenever possible. Though the reproductions in this book are in black and white, I insist that student cartoons be in color. I also look for effort, which can usually be seen in the details.

In this book, you will find 40 sample cartoons. Most of these were dawn by 10-year-olds. There is also a brief explanation of each of the historical events that inspired the cartoons and easy-to-follow assignments. I think you will find, as I have, that students eagerly embrace the challenge of drawing 35–40 history cartoons over the course of the school year. Indeed, by November, you will probably begin hearing the question, "What is the cartoon for this week?" And the walls and bulletin boards in your classroom will become a constantly changing art gallery.

The Settling of Jamestown

The History

In late December 1606, on the docks of the River Thames, near London, 104 Englishmen and boys prepared to sail across the Atlantic Ocean to the "New World." Their ships were named the *Susan Constant*, the *Discovery*, and the *Godspeed*. This expedition had been paid for by a group of investors known as The London Company. These investors hoped that when the Englishmen arrived in Virginia, they would find as much gold as the Spanish had found in Mexico nearly 90 years before. That would mean big profits for everyone.

The Englishmen made it across the ocean. They explored the Chesapeake Bay, where they feasted on oysters. Then, near a river that they named after King James, these men started the first permanent English settlement in the "New World." They called this settlement Jamestown, of course. More ships arrived and the population of Jamestown swelled to 500. But, alas, the English found no gold. And in the winter of 1609, the Powhatan Indians surrounded the fort at Jamestown and tried to starve them. One of the settlers wrote, "Many of our men this Starving Time did run away unto the savages, whom we never heard of after." By May, 1610, only 60 were alive, and they were ready to leave.

The Assignment

Think of good things going bad, such as fresh fruit becoming rotten, flowers wilting, or ice cream melting. Use one of these (or one of your own) as a metaphor to represent the colonists' hope of finding gold, food, and peace, and the reality of no gold, no food, and war. Divide your paper in half and show the hope on one side and the reality on the other.

Possible Title

Jamestown: The Dream Becomes a Nightmare

Pocahontas

The History

Pocahontas, the daughter of the Powhatan chief, was about 12 years old when the Englishmen came to Virginia. In the early days of the Jamestown settlement, she brought food to the visitors. She got to know their 28-year-old leader, whose name was John Smith. Pocahontas liked Smith; he was intelligent, curious, and fearless. Legend has it that when Smith was captured by the Powhatan and about to be killed, she saved his life. In many popular versions of the story, John Smith and Pocahontas are often romantically involved but the truth is that he was more like an uncle to her.

When Smith went back to England after being burned in a gunpowder explosion, Pocahontas met and fell in love with a tobacco farmer named John Rolfe. Their marriage in 1614 was followed by eight years of peace between the Englishmen and the Native Americans. With her husband and her new baby, Thomas, Pocahontas went to England in 1616. There people called her by her new name, Rebecca. In London, this Indian princess charmed everyone, including King James. People pointed to her when she walked down the street. Pocahontas was a celebrity. But she wondered why John Smith hadn't come to see her. When Smith finally did show up, after weeks had passed, she told him she had been hurt by his absence. He wasn't sure what to say to this Indian girl who now looked like a proper Englishwoman.

Pocahontas started back to America in 1617, but got so sick that her husband took her off the boat. She died of smallpox and was buried near London. She was only 22.

The Assignment

Do additional research on Pocahontas. (You will find that her real name was Matoax. What does it mean?) Think about the conflicts in her life that could be turned into headlines. Then glue a magazine logo onto your paper and turn Pocahontas into the cover story.

Possible Title

The Princess From Across the Sea

Virginia, 1619

The History

The year 1619 brought many changes to Virginia. In that year, the first Africans arrived. The first lawmakers were elected to Virginia's Legislature, the House of Burgesses. Polish glassmakers led the first strike in the future United States and demanded the same rights as Englishmen. For the first time, English settlers were allowed to own land. And perhaps most importantly, the first European women arrived in the New World. Permanent homes and families would not be far behind. Clearly the English were here to stay.

The Assignment

Imagine you're the publisher and writer of a Virginia newspaper that comes out once a year. Design the front page of your paper to include articles about the five significant events of 1619. Think of some supporting details that might follow your topic sentences. Imagine the scene at the docks when the women arrived. Discuss the qualifications for serving in the House of Burgesses. Contrast African slaves with slaves of ancient times, and comment on why slaves were brought to Virginia. Illustrate at least two of the articles.

Possible Title

The 1619 News

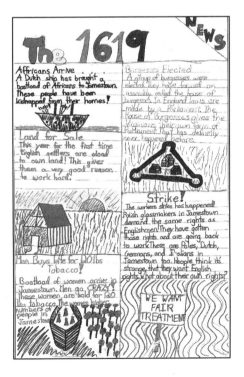

Slavery in the "New World"

The History

The Spanish were the first to bring African slaves to the New World. In the late 1400s, they shipped slaves to the West Indies to plant and cut sugar cane. The first boatload of Africans arrived in Jamestown in 1619. During the next two centuries, millions of Africans were taken from their homelands, packed into overcrowded slave ships and taken to America where they were auctioned to plantation owners. Often, families were separated. In 1800, the population of America was 5.3 million—and over one-fifth were slaves. It was legal to bring slaves into the country until 1808, but many more were smuggled in after that. Slaves had no rights and received no pay. Slaves and children of slave mothers were never set free. Most of the slaves came from West Africa, an area that had been rich in art, music, architecture, and agriculture. The slave trade dealt a severe blow to many of these flourishing societies.

The Assignment

Think of a symbol for a flourishing society. You might use a blooming flower, a clear river, or a salmon leaping upstream. Label this "African Society." Then think of a threat to the flower, river, salmon, or other symbol you choose. Label this "Slave Traders."

Possible Title

The Shame of Slavery

Fragile Relationships in the "New World"

The History

Relations between Native Americans and the newly-arrived Europeans followed a pattern. In the beginning there was usually peace. Bullets were sometimes fired or arrows shot, but this rarely led to massacres or war. Then something happened to disrupt this fragile relationship. In Virginia, John Smith was burned in a gunpowder explosion and had to go back to England. His leadership skills were sorely missed. The settlers who were left behind angered the Powhatan, who responded by trying to starve them. Then in a massacre in 1622, 350 men and women in Jamestown were killed.

In Massachusetts, peace lasted as long as Chief Massasoit was alive. He was the Wampanoag Chief who in 1621 sat down for a Thanksgiving feast with the Pilgrims. After Massasoit's death, the simmering anger between the two different cultures bubbled up and King Philip's War began.

The Assignment

Divide your paper in half. Label the left half "The First Generation." Label the right half "The Second Generation." Think of how you might depict a good relationship gone bad. You might also think in terms of something turning from sweet to sour or fresh to rotten. Use the words *pilgrims*, *Chief Massasoit*, *Wampanoag*, and *King Philip's War* in your illustration.

Possible Title

Generation Gap

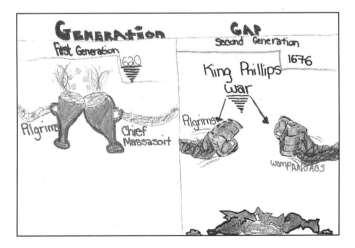

The Roots of Democracy

The History

When English settlers first came to the shores of Virginia and Massachusetts, survival was foremost on their minds. But they were also concerned with establishing a set of rules for their new societies. In Virginia in 1607, one of the first rules that Governor John Smith laid down was "Those who don't work won't eat." And even before the *Mayflower* landed at Plymouth in 1620, William Bradford and his fellow Pilgrims wrote the *Mayflower Compact*, which established a governing body to enact laws "for the general good of the colony."

In Virginia, the lawmakers, known as representatives, met in the House of Burgesses. In New England, there were town meetings in which every citizen could be heard. This kind of government only works in a small town that has a big meeting house. Some rich, powerful people feared democracy (which means "government by the people.") They didn't want to give power to a mob of ordinary citizens. But in the end, ordinary citizens would have their say.

The Assignment

Think of a new idea taking root, a new home being built, plants pushing their way up through the soil and toward the sunlight, or birds building a nest. Label the plants or birds "Virginia House of Burgesses," "Mayflower Compact," and "New England Town Meetings." Label the soil or the nest "American Colonies."

Possible Title

Democracy Takes Root in the "New World"

The Legacy of the Puritans

The History

In 1630, the first Puritan ship, the *Arbella*, left England for the "New World." By year's end, 1,000 Puritans had landed in New England. They brought with them a charter written by lawyers and approved by King Charles. The charter allowed the colonists to govern themselves.

The Puritans were better educated and had more money than the Pilgrims (who had arrived ten years earlier). In 1636, the Puritans built the first college in the American colonies and named it Harvard. All Puritan children had to know how to read the Bible and so, in 1647, a law was passed requiring every town with more than 50 inhabitants to hire a schoolteacher. This was the beginning of public education in America.

The Puritans had many rules that were meant to control people's behavior—especially on the Sabbath. You could be punished for cooking, running, or shaving on Sunday. One man was put in the stocks for kissing his wife on that holy day. These rules were called Blue Laws, because the Puritans wrote them in books bound in blue paper.

One man who thought the Puritans were too strict was a Puritan minister named Roger Williams. He believed that each person should be able to choose his or her own religion. Years later, that idea would become part of America's Bill of Rights.

The Assignment

Think of a foundation, building blocks, puppies, or flower buds—anything that will grow into something bigger. Draw five of these little things and label them "Harvard—1636," "Literacy," "Public Education," "Blue Laws," and "Roger Williams." If a full-grown dog is caring for her puppies, label her "Puritans."

Possible Title

The Puritan Legacy

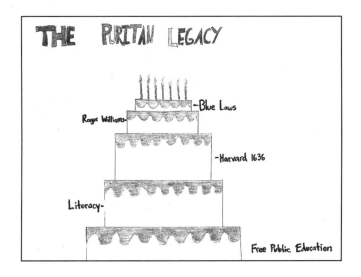

Separation of Church and State

The History

Roger Williams was a Puritan minister who believed that land should not be taken from the Indians. He believed that killing in the name of Christianity was sinful. And he believed that each person should be free to choose his own religion with no interference from the government. When the Puritan leaders decided to ship Williams back to England, he fled Massachusetts. Only with help from the Narragansett Indians was he able to survive the winter of 1636. Later he bought land from the Indians and started a colony called Providence. It became the capital of Rhode Island, and that colony attracted people who, because of their religion, had been persecuted elsewhere. Soon Rhode Island was home to Quakers, Jews, and even atheists (who don't believe in any god). Williams made sure there would be no connection between churches or synagogues and the government. Since the government is sometimes called "the state" this idea was called "the separation of church and state."

The Assignment

Think of two halves of something that usually form a whole, but in this case they are being separated. Label the two halves "Church" and "State." Label the object that is separating them "Roger Williams."

Possible Title

The Separation of Church and State

Penn's Woods

The History

King Charles II (also known as "The Merry Monarch") had borrowed quite a bit of money from William Penn's father. When his father died, William asked the king to repay his debt with land in colonial America. As a result, in 1681 Penn received a colony bigger than England. King Charles named it Pennsylvania, which means Penn's woods. Penn, who was a Quaker, hoped his colony would become a place of peace, goodness, and brotherly love. Quakers were *pacifists* (they didn't think fighting and wars should be used to solve problems). As a result, Indians received better treatment in Pennsylvania than they did in most other colonies. People of all nations and all religions were welcome in Pennsylvania. Germans, Swedes, Finns, Dutch, and English poured into the new colony. In 1800, Philadelphia, Pennsylvania, was the largest city in the colonies (with a population of 70,000). Two great American documents were written there: The Declaration of Independence (1776) and The Constitution (1787).

The Assignment

Divide your paper in half. On top of the left half, write "One Man's Gift." Now, think of something you might give to a man—socks, perhaps, or a necktie or a bottle of cologne. Draw that on the left side of the paper. On the top of the right half, write "Another Man's Gift" and draw William Penn and his gift of Pennsylvania.

Possible Title

Penn's Woods

The Salem Witch Trials

The History

In 1692, in the town of Salem, Massachusetts, over 100 people were put on trial and accused of being witches. Twenty of them (and two dogs!) were put to death. This happened partly because, in the 16th and 17th centuries, people all over the world believed that witches really were flying around on broomsticks, squeezing through keyholes, killing sheep, and sinking ships. Witches were blamed for evil everywhere in the world.

In Salem, a servant named Tituba, who came from the Caribbean island of Barbados, would tell scary stories to two young Salem girls, Elizabeth Parris and Abigail Williams. After hearing these tales, the girls began barking like dogs, meowing like cats, and shouting out in church. Most likely they were just having a little fun and trying to get some attention, but the townsfolk were sure the girls had been bewitched. Elizabeth and Abigail decided to play along and accused Tituba and two old women of being witches. The women were arrested. Seeing the power they suddenly had, the girls began accusing others of being witches. The girls finally went too far when they accused the Reverend John Hale's wife, Sarah, of being a witch. People began to wonder if the girls had been wrong all along, but by then it was too late. Samuel Sewall, one of the judges who had sentenced several "witches" to death, made a public apology for all the wrongs that been done to decent, law abiding citizens.

The Assignment

Pretend the Salem Witch Trials is the name of a movie. Design a movie poster that includes the headline: Coming Soon to a Courthouse Near You! Include the names of the "stars"—Tituba, Judge Sewall, Sarah Hale, and Elizabeth Parris and Abigail Williams. Think about including a promotional give-a-way, such as: Free Brooms to the First 30 Spectators. And, of course, include comments from the critics.

Possible Title

The Salem Witch Trials

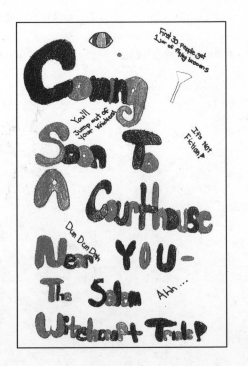

Freedom of the Press

The History

On a hot, August morning in 1735, a New York newspaper publisher named Peter Zenger was put on trial. He was accused of publishing articles in his *New York Weekly Journal* that were critical of William Cosby, the royal governor of New York. The articles accused Cosby of taking bribes and rigging elections. Cosby's lawyer said that Zenger was guilty of libel and should be sent to jail.

In those days, British subjects, including all of the colonists, could be accused of libel if they said anything bad about the King of Great Britain—even if what they said was true! Because Cosby was the king's governor in New York, his lawyer said that he should be treated the same as the king would be.

Zenger's lawyer was Andrew Hamilton. He was from Philadelphia and was considered the finest lawyer in the colonies. When Hamilton addressed the jury, he said that free men have a right to complain when hurt and that they have a right to oppose arbitrary power by speaking and writing truths. There is no libel if the truth is told. In a unanimous decision they reached in only 10 minutes, the jury ended up agreeing with Hamilton and Zenger was found not guilty. The right to publish the truth, "freedom of the press," would later be included in our Bill of Rights.

The Assignment

Think of a person or animal trying to seek shelter from wind, rain, or another threat from Mother Nature. Label this person or animal "Governor Cosby." Label the rain or wind "The Truth." Make "The Truth" so powerful that it's obvious that Cosby can't hide for long. For example, Hamilton can grab the umbrella from Cosby so he'll be soaked by "the truth."

Possible Title

Peter Zenger Fights for Freedom of the Press

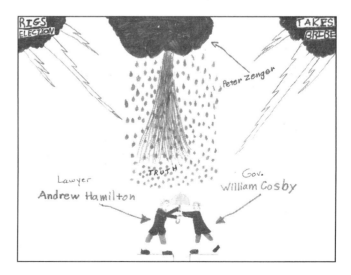

Germs: More Deadly Than Guns

The History

While European guns and swords killed many Native Americans, the biggest killer by far was an invisible one. Germs brought across the Atlantic by the early explorers, and later by the settlers and their animals, wiped out entire Native American villages and tribes. The Native Americans had no natural immunity to these diseases, which included smallpox, measles, and influenza. Evidence now suggests that when Columbus arrived in 1492, there might have been close to 20 million Native Americans in North America. Two centuries later, the Native American population had declined (according to some estimates) by 95 percent. And things did not improve with time. In North Dakota in 1837, 345 years after Columbus landed, a Mandan village was infected with smallpox by men who came up the Missouri River from St. Louis. Within a few weeks, the population of the village fell from 2,000 to 40.

The Assignment

Think of a symbol for the Native Americans, perhaps a hawk or mountain peak. Then think of something that could threaten that hawk or mountain peak. Label your Native American symbol. And label the threat "Disease" or "Smallpox."

Possible Title

What Killed More Indians Than Guns?

The French and Indian War

The History

From 1754 to 1760, Great Britain and France fought a war that became known as the French and Indian War. This was the final war in a series of conflicts in North America between the British and French for territorial control—and the North American chapter of the larger Seven Years' War, which was fought in Europe, as well as India.

The battlefields of the French and Indian War were in New York, Pennsylvania, and Canada. The winner would control a huge chunk of North America, including the land west of Pittsburgh (known as the Ohio Valley), the Great Lakes, and the St. Lawrence River. All the Indian tribes in this area had to choose sides in this war. Most of them chose to side with the French, including the Abenaki, the Ottawa, the Ojibwa, the Caughnawaga, the Winnebago, the Menominee, and the Potawatami. Only the Iroquois sided with the British.

In 1763, the British and the French signed the Treaty of Paris that ultimately ended the French and Indian War. The French holdings in North America were reduced to two tiny islands off the coast of Canada. The British had won all the land from the east coast to the Mississippi River and as a result, Great Britain now ruled over an empire that rivaled in size and power the Roman Empire of ancient days. The jewel of this empire was America's thirteen colonies that stretched from New Hampshire to Georgia and provided Great Britain with fish, fur, lumber, tobacco, indigo, rice, figs, pitch, and other valuable products.

The Assignment

Think of two adversaries fighting over one very valuable prize. Label the participants and the prize.

Possible Title

Great Britain Versus France

The Seeds of Revolution

The History

To help pay off debts that had mounted during the waging of the French and Indian War, the British government decided to tax the 13 American colonies. The Stamp Tax, levied in 1765, made it mandatory for colonists to buy a British stamp for every piece of printed paper they used. Later, other taxes were levied on glass, paint, and tea. Some colonists began to speak out against these taxes, and against the general notion of being taxed without being consulted beforehand. "No taxation without representation" became the rallying cry of the resistance movement. The men who led this resistance were called "firebrands" because they were stoking the fires of dissent and, ultimately, revolution. Three of the better-known firebrands were Sam Adams, Thomas Paine, and Patrick Henry.

The Assignment

Think of pests or little things that can get under your skin. Think about how these irritants could trouble an otherwise intimidating figure. Include the names of the firebrands and some of their famous words. Be sure to label the target of their anger.

Possible Title

Three Firebrands Annoy George III

The Shot Heard 'Round the World

The History

On the morning of April 19, 1775, British regulars confronted armed colonists on the village green in Lexington, Massachusetts. No one knows who fired first, but when the smoke cleared, eight colonists lay dead and one British soldier was wounded. The British then marched on toward Concord, Massachusetts, where they looked for the gunpowder the colonists had stored there. When they found none, the British ate breakfast, set a few gun carriages on fire, and marched back toward Boston. At the Old North Bridge, outside of Concord, they were confronted by a force of Minutemen. Shots were fired. Of the eight British officers at the North Bridge, four were wounded. Three privates were killed. Then, amazingly, the British soldiers turned and fled. A ragtag bunch of farmers had routed the best trained soldiers in the world. One British soldier wrote of the American militia, "The weight of their fire was such that we were obliged to give way, then to run." Later, poet Ralph Waldo Emerson wrote of this battle:

> By the rude bridge that arched the flood,
> Their flag to April's breeze unfurled,
> Here once the embattled farmers stood,
> And fired the shot heard 'round the world.

The Assignment

Take the poetic phrase, "The shot heard 'round the world," and illustrate it. One approach would be to draw a map and put big ears in such cities as Boston, New York, Philadelphia, Charleston, London, Paris, and Sydney. Think of a way you might depict the battle at Concord without actually drawing soldiers.

Possible Title

The Shot Heard 'Round the World

The Declaration of Independence

The History

In the summer of 1776, over a year after the confrontations at Lexington and Concord, after the bloodless capture of Fort Ticonderoga, and the bloody Battle of Bunker Hill, the Second Continental Congress met in Philadelphia. John Adams of Massachusetts spurred the delegates to approve a break from Great Britain. Then he and Ben Franklin turned to the delegate from Virginia, Thomas Jefferson, and asked him to write the reasons why the American colonies were rebelling from the Mother Country. Jefferson went to write in his rented room. Several days and many drafts later, he returned with a document in which he listed a number of reasons why the colonies should rebel. "King George III," wrote Jefferson, "has kept among us, in times of peace, standing armies without the consent of our legislatures. He has cut off our trade with all parts of the world, he has imposed taxes without our consent, he has deprived us, in many cases, of the benefits of trial by jury." Before listing these abuses however, Jefferson wrote a paragraph that would ring down through the ages. It reads, in part,

> *We hold these truths to be self-evident, that all Men are created equal, that they are endowed by their Creator with certain unalienable Rights, that among these are Life, Liberty, and the Pursuit of Happiness.*

On July 4, 1776, the members of the Second Continental Congress approved this Declaration of Independence.

The Assignment

First, make sure you understand what "self-evident," "endowed by their Creator," and "unalienable" mean. Then have some fun with this section of the Declaration of Independence. Think of another creature you might substitute for "men." Try cows, chickens, or snails. Then consider what these creatures might declare as their unalienable rights. Rewrite and illustrate your new Declaration of Independence.

Possible Title

Declaration of Animal Independence

We hold these truths to be self-evident, that all cows are created equal, that they are endowed by their Creator with certain unalienable Rights, that among these are Life, Liberty and the pursuit of good grass.

The Battle for New York

The History

In the summer of 1776, British soldiers landed in New York. A New Yorker named Daniel McCurtin described what he saw as he looked out his window. "I spied as I peeped out something resembling a wood of pine trees. The whole bay was full of shipping . . . I thought all London was afloat."

Washington's army was in New York to take on the British, which would prove to be a frightening encounter. The colonial army was made up of citizen-soldiers who were untrained, underpaid, poorly clothed, and underfed. They were also badly outnumbered by a British army made up of experienced, professional soldiers with spiffy uniforms and the latest weapons. Washington would need some luck merely to survive.

Meanwhile, France was awaiting news of these early battles. Silas Deane, a Connecticut merchant, arrived in Paris in July 1776, and tried to convince the French to come to the aid of the colonies. The French were slow to commit. They didn't want to lose another war to the British.

The Assignment

Think about an awesome champion versus a little challenger. Or think about an example of the power of nature: a tidal wave versus a rowboat, a towering mountain peak versus a lone climber. Or think about the animal kingdom: a cat versus a mouse. Your two symbols should be labeled "British Army" and "Washington and His Citizen-Soldiers." And off to the side there should be an observer labeled "The French." This observer should have an object in hand that could help the challenger, such as a life preserver, a rope, or boxing gloves.

Possible Title

The Battle for New York—1776

The Battle of Saratoga

The History

By the summer of 1777, the British were ready to march south from Canada. Their strategy was to take control of the Hudson River and cut New England and New York off from the other colonies. The general who would lead the British Army was John Burgoyne.

In Saratoga, a small town on the Hudson just north of Albany, General Horatio Gates and his American forces waited. Gates was aided by Colonel Thaddeus Kosciuszko (kush-CHOO-shko), who'd come from Poland to help the Americans. He was a military engineer, and he had placed cannons on the bluffs around Saratoga. In addition, farmers from New York and Massachusetts poured into the area, and soon the American force was triple the size of Burgoyne's army. The British lost about 600 soldiers during the battle. On October 17, 1777, Burgoyne and his mighty army surrendered. This victory finally convinced the French to join the war on the American side.

The Assignment

Divide your paper in half. On the left side, draw a wilted plant or something else that is not in good condition. Label this plant "The American Army Before Saratoga." On the right side of the paper add a needed element such as fertilizer or water. Label that element "The French." Label the healthy plant "The American Army After Saratoga."

Possible Title

The French Arrive After Saratoga

The Battle of Yorktown

The History

During the Revolutionary War, the British had more men, more guns, and more experience than the colonists did. Subsequently, they won more battles than did the Americans; and yet, they lost the war. Why? The Americans and their French allies conspired to trap the entire British army at Yorktown, Virginia. They accomplished this feat by executing a daring military strategy that required perfect timing, superb communication, and good weather. Admiral de Grasse and the French fleet sailed over a thousand miles from Haiti to Virginia. Washington's army and French troops led by General Rochambeau left Rhode Island and marched 500 miles south. Incredibly, de Grasse, Washington, and Rochambeau arrived at Yorktown simultaneously. de Grasse's ships set up a blockade. As a result, British General Cornwallis was unable to resupply his army. Washington and Rochambeau attacked the weakened British army from the west. When the British surrendered, the army band played an old English nursery tune called "The World Turned Upside Down."

The Assignment

Think of an underdog defeating an overwhelming favorite. Or think of prey triumphing over a predator. Label the two combatants. Include the word "Yorktown" and the names of the generals.

Possible Title

The World Turned Upside Down

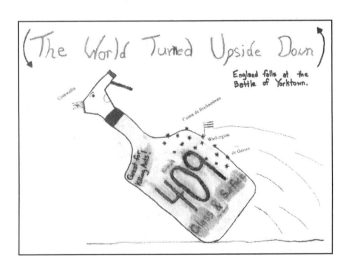

The Northwest Ordinance

The History

From 1781–1789, the 13 American states were held together by a document called the Articles of Confederation. It was written in 1776, but not ratified until 1781. The Articles of Confederation defined a new form of government that gave every state one vote, requiring nine "yes" votes before a proposal became a law.

One of the few successful pieces of legislation passed during this period was the Northwest Ordinance of 1787. This law laid out the steps for incorporating the Northwest Territories into the new country. The future states of Ohio, Indiana, Michigan, Wisconsin, and Minnesota would be carved out of this area, becoming full-fledged states under the provisions of this new law. Citizens governed by the Northwest Ordinance had a guaranteed freedom of religion, habeas corpus, and trial by jury. The ordinance also banned slavery in these territories (and later, states).

The Assignment

Consider the idea of new members joining an established club. In the case, a "club" could be anything from a salad bowl to a pod of whales. Label the club's established members and its new members. Include the name of the law that allowed the smooth transition of territories into statehood and three rights guaranteed to their citizens.

Possible Title

Five Territories Join the U.S.A.

The Constitutional Convention

The History

By May 1787, 11 years after the Declaration of Independence, America was in trouble. Even though the country was called the United States of America, it was, in fact, a collection of 13 separate states, fighting with each other over boundaries, taxes, and river navigation. States printed their own money, and nine states even had their own navies. The little states feared the big states, and the big states could not protect the citizens on their western borders. Congress had no power to collect taxes, so it couldn't pay soldiers or sailors. Washington, in despair, wrote, "Thirteen sovereign states pulling against each . . . other will soon bring ruin on the whole."

Two men who wanted to take the country in a more unified direction were James Madison and Alexander Hamilton. As early as 1780, Hamilton had written that it was impossible to govern 13 sovereign states. There was only one way to find a remedy: to call a convention of all the states. Madison wrote to men in other states and asked them to appoint delegates to the Constitutional Convention. Fifty-five of America's most notable citizens would come and go during that long, hot summer of 1787. By September, most would sign a new document called The Constitution of the United States.

The Assignment

Think of men or animals rounding up other animals. One possibility is to draw two sheep dogs and label them "Madison" and "Hamilton." Draw them herding sheep into a pen and label the pen "Constitutional Convention—1787." Label the sheep with names of delegates such as "Edmund Randolph," "Benjamin Franklin," "Gouverneur Morris," "George Washington," "William Paterson," "Roger Sherman," "George Mason," "Rufus King," and "James Wilson."

Possible Title

James Madison and Alexander Hamilton Push for a New Form of Government

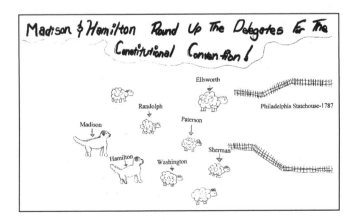

A New Form of Government

The History

In June 1787, delegates to the Constitutional Convention confronted their biggest obstacle. How should the 13 states be represented in the new legislature? James Madison's Virginia Plan called for the legislature to have two houses (an upper and a lower) with the big states having the most representatives in both houses. William Paterson of New Jersey said the small states would never consent to such a system. New Jersey's delegates declared it would not be "safe" to allow Virginia 16 times as many votes as Delaware. So Paterson proposed the New Jersey Plan, which proposed a one-house legislature to which each state would send an equal number of representatives. That plan was defeated.

In the midst of this heated debate, Roger Sherman of Connecticut proposed a compromise: create a legislature comprised of two houses with members chosen by two different methods. In the lower house (the House of Representatives) the number of representatives would be based on the population of the state. In the upper house (the Senate) the number of representatives would be equal. That plan gave small states more power in the upper house, and it made sure the big states would control the lower house. The Sherman Plan, also known as The Connecticut Compromise, was passed by the delegates. Had it not passed, the Constitutional Convention might have collapsed that June.

The Assignment

Bring together two traditional adversaries, for example, a cat and dog. Label the cat "Little States" and label the dog "Big States." Label the object that brings them together "The Sherman Plan." If it's food that brings them together, you might also write the following on the bag of food: "Proportional Representation in the House, Equal Representation in the Senate."

Possible Title

Roger Sherman's Plan Saves the Constitutional Convention

Read ★ Draw ★ Remember American History Activities

Writing the Constitution

The History

During the last days of the Constitutional Convention in September 1787, Gouverneur Morris, the Pennsylvania delegate, was given the job of writing the final draft of the Constitution. He sat down and wrote these words: "We the people of the United States . . ." The first draft of the preamble had started with the words: "We the undersigned delegates of the states of New Hampshire, Massachusetts . . ." and so on. But Morris believed that Rhode Island and New York would not want to be named as sponsors of the Constitution. The smallest state did not want a new form of government under which it might lose power to the bigger states—and, therefore, sent no delegates to the convention. New York also preferred the old form of government—two of its three delegates went home in a huff halfway through the convention. Morris avoided naming any of the states. He also deleted all references to slavery. Otherwise, he determined, many delegates from southern states would not have signed the document. He continued writing ". . . in order to form a more perfect union, establish justice, insure domestic tranquility, provide for the common defense, promote the general welfare, and secure the blessings of liberty to ourselves and our posterity, do ordain and establish this Constitution for the United States of America."

After writing the preamble, Morris took the 23 articles before him and shrunk them into seven, thus creating a shorter, reader-friendly document that is still widely quoted over 200 years later. Madison wrote, "The finish given to the style of the Constitution belongs to the pen of Mr. Morris." As for Madison, he was responsible for much of the substance of the Constitution and for the record keeping. Of the 55 men who came and went that summer, 39 signed the document and it was then sent to the states. Nine states would have to ratify the Constitution before it would become the supreme law of the land.

The Assignment

Divide your paper into eighths. At the top of each section, write a phrase from the preamble to the Constitution. Then either illustrate that phrase or find a picture from a magazine that reinforces the theme of the phrase.

Possible Title

The Preamble to the Constitution

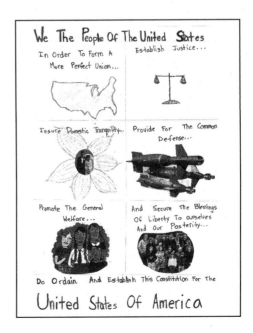

We The People Of The United States
In Order To Form A More Perfect Union...
Establish Justice...
Insure Domestic Tranquility...
Provide For The Common Defense...
Promote The General Welfare...
And Secure The Blessings Of Liberty To ourselves And Our Posterity...
Do Ordain And Establish This Constitution For The
United States Of America

Recipe for Ratification

The History

The writers (or framers) of the Constitution knew that they could not get all 13 states to ratify (or approve) the new document. So they wisely declared that the Constitution would become the law of the land if only nine states would ratify it. The states then held their own ratification conventions, during which men spoke about the benefits and the dangers of this new form of government. The most dramatic debate took place in Richmond, Virginia. Here, in June 1788, Patrick Henry stood and shouted, "I look on [the Constitution] as the most fatal plan that could possibly be conceived to enslave a free people." Henry got so excited he twirled the wig around on his head. James Madison tried to answer all of Henry's criticisms, and when Madison got tired (and went home sick) Edmund Randolph took on Henry. This was a surprise, because Randolph was one of the delegates who would not sign the Constitution in Philadelphia. Randolph said that he had since changed his mind and was now ready to ratify under one condition: A Bill of Rights had to be added to the Constitution after it was ratified. Enough delegates in Richmond agreed with Randolph to make the final vote 89–79 in favor of ratification. The Bill of Rights would be added by the first Congress in 1791.

The Assignment

Divide your paper in half. Think of a dessert that is missing its final ingredient, for example, a slice of pie without the ice cream or a cake without icing. Or consider french fries without ketchup or peanut butter without jelly. On the left half of your paper, draw the food with the missing ingredient. Label it "The Constitution—1787" and then circle it and put a diagonal line through the circle. On the right half, draw the food with the added ingredient. Label the food "The Constitution—1791," and label the added ingredient "The Bill of Rights."

Possible Title

Recipe for Ratification

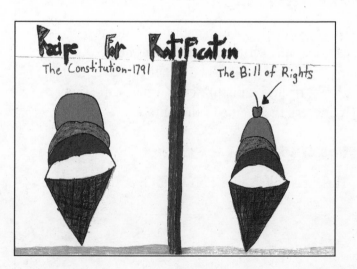

The Alien and Sedition Acts

The History

In 1798, the Congress passed four laws called the Alien and Sedition Acts. President Adams signed them and they become law. One of these acts, the Naturalization Act, made it difficult for foreigners to become U.S. citizens. Another, the Alien Act, allowed the President to toss anyone he wanted out of the country. The Sedition Act made it a crime to criticize the President or members of Congress, and some people were arrested for speaking out. One of them was Benjamin Franklin's grandson.

Article 1 of the Bill of Rights says, "Congress shall make no law respecting an establishment of religion, or prohibiting the free exercise thereof; or abridging the freedom of speech, or of the press . . ." And yet, the Sedition Act was doing just that. In the legislatures of Virginia and Kentucky, men rose and said their states would not enforce such laws. When John Adams ran for reelection, he lost to Thomas Jefferson. One reason for the defeat was his support of the Alien and Sedition Acts. Jefferson pardoned everyone convicted under the Sedition Act.

The Assignment

Think of a creature or a plant getting threatened or attacked. Label the creature or plant "The Bill of Rights." Label the threat "The Alien and Sedition Acts."

Possible Title

A Sad Day in American History

America's Population Grows

The History

The Native Americans and the Europeans had very different views about how land should be used. The Native Americans had little use for private property and fences. For the most part, they left the land and the trees undisturbed. For them, the wilderness was a sacred place, home of clean water, fruit trees, medicinal plants, and animal habitats. Some accounts suggest that before Columbus arrived in 1492, there were so many trees in the "New World" that a squirrel could travel from the Atlantic Ocean to the Mississippi River and never touch the ground.

The English were less interested in preservation in their colony and more interested in town building and profit making. For them timber was the ideal natural resource. It could be used to build homes, and it could also be exported to England to build more ships for its growing navy. On the east coast of America, tens of thousands of acres were cleared so that towns and crops could grow, cattle could graze, and money could be made.

By 1800, the population of America's cities was swelling and Mother Nature was in retreat.

The Assignment

Divide your paper in half. On the left half, write the heading "America Before 1492." Draw a scene of Mother Nature in all her glory. Label the various plants, trees, and animals with the names of the east coast Native American tribes. On the right half, write the heading "America in 1800." Draw a scene in which little is left of Mother Nature except four sorry-looking reminders. These reminders should be labeled "Philadelphia—70,000," "New York—60,000," "Boston—25,000," and "Charleston—24,000."

Possible Title

America's Changing Landscape

John Marshall and the Supreme Court

The History

John Marshall was the fourth chief justice of the United States Supreme Court. He served in that job from 1801 to 1835. The chief justices before him had been uncertain about what role the Supreme Court should play in the new nation. As a result the judicial branch had been the weakest of the three branches of government. Marshall, however, had no uncertainty. He said it was the role of the court to review all laws and decide if they fit within the guidelines of the United States Constitution. That meant that if a law was passed by the two houses of the legislative branch and signed by the President it could still be declared unconstitutional by Marshall and his fellow justices. This is called judicial review, because it allows the judicial branch to review, interpret, and nullify a law. By doing this, the judicial branch was able to protect the rights of the American people—even from Congress and the President. Today the Supreme Court continues to interpret the law and hand down opinions that affect millions of Americans.

The Assignment

Draw a contraption with lots of pulleys and gears into which big boxes move on a conveyor belt. Label the boxes "Laws Passed By Congress and Signed by the President." Label the contraption "Judicial Review." In a chair that's connected to the contraption, draw a man who's working some levers. Label this man "Chief Justice John Marshall." Draw objects coming out of the contraption as they either slide onto a wagon or are shot into a trashcan. On the side of the wagon, write "Constitutional." On the trashcan, write "Unconstitutional."

Possible Title

John Marshall Empowers the Supreme Court

The Louisiana Purchase

The History

Sometime during the spring of 1803, Napolean Bonaparte, Emperor of France, decided to sell the Louisiana Territory to the United States. This vast territory stretched from the Mississippi River to the Rocky Mountains and from the Gulf of Mexico to the Canadian border.

Napolean had three reasons for selling the land. First, his army of 30,000 was trying to stop a slave revolt on the French island of Haiti (then called St. Domingue), and he didn't have enough troops available to defend Louisiana, too. Second, he needed cash because he wanted to fight the British and take Egypt from them. Third, he wanted to make America more powerful so England would have to deal with another strong rival.

Napolean negotiated with two American envoys in Paris, Robert Livingston and James Monroe (who would later become President). Napolean first asked for $22,500,000. Livingston and Monroe offered $8,000,000. They finally settled on a price of $15,000,000. When President Jefferson heard about the purchase, he sent Meriwether Lewis and William Clark to explore this land and find out what he had just bought.

The Assignment

Draw a vehicle or a pack animal (such as a donkey or a camel). Now pile high atop that vehicle or animal a heavy load. Label this load "The Louisiana Purchase." Label the vehicle or animal "United States." Put two men in the vehicle or atop the animal. Label these men "Lewis" and "Clark." If you have access to the Internet, you can download a picture of Napoleon. If not, you can draw him—perhaps running after the vehicle or animal waving a $15,000,000 receipt.

Possible Title

America Doubles Its Size

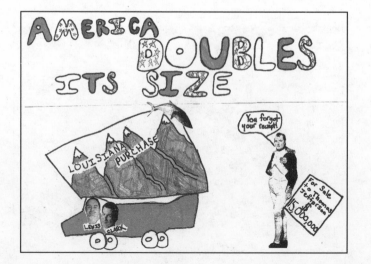

America Harnesses the Power of Steam

The History

In 1807, Robert Fulton built a steamboat that he called the *Clermont*. This boat was able to sail up the Hudson River from New York to Albany in 32 hours. Before Fulton's invention, traveling upriver against the current required using either paddle or poles to push off from the river bottom, or being pulled by horses or lots of men. By 1820, there were 60 steamboats on the Mississippi. By 1860, there were nearly one thousand.

Steam was also used by Peter Cooper to power *Tom Thumb*, the locomotive that he built in 1830. Trains could carry heavier loads than stagecoaches and could travel year round, which wasn't possible on canals because in winter the water froze. By 1840, there were more than 3,000 miles of railroad tracks in America. British novelist Charles Dickens visited the United States and took a train ride in 1842. He later wrote,

> On it whirls headlong, dives through the woods again, emerges in the light, clatters over frail arches, rumbles upon the heavy ground, shoots beneath a wooden bridge . . . suddenly awakens all the slumbering echoes in the main street of a large town, and dashes on haphazard, pell-mell, neck-or-nothing, down the middle of the road.

The Assignment

Divide your paper in half. On the left half, draw a teakettle with steam coming out. Draw a man raising his index finger and in a speech bubble, write "That gives me an idea." Label the man "Robert Fulton" or "Peter Cooper." On the right half, draw a steamboat or a locomotive. Label the steamboat "The Clermont—1807," or label the locomotive "Tom Thumb—1830." Show the steam emerging from the smokestack on the boat or the train engine.

Possible Title

America Harnesses Steam Power

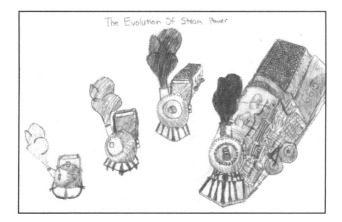

The Erie Canal

The History

When Thomas Jefferson heard of plans to build the Erie Canal, he said, "It's little short of madness to talk of making a canal of 350 miles through the wilderness." And yet, in 1825, when this artificial waterway was completed, it connected the Hudson River to the Great Lakes. The canal was four feet deep and 40 feet wide. The boats were pulled by horses or mules that walked on towpaths next to the canal. Some of the boats traveled along at four miles an hour. A passenger on such a boat would pay 5 cents a mile. Along the route there were 83 locks that were built to overcome the 571-foot difference between the level of the Hudson River and the level of Lake Erie. These locks were engineering marvels. Inside these enclosed chambers, the water would be raised so the boats could float over a hill and then, on the other side, the water—and thus boats—would be lowered. Governor DeWitt Clinton took the first ride on the canal. He rode from Buffalo to New York City in nine days.

The Erie Canal would have a dramatic impact on the American economy. For example, thirty years after the Erie Canal was built, the cost of shipping grain via waterway from Buffalo to New York City had been reduced by over $90 per ton. Timber, pelts, and coal could also be shipped inexpensively, and in large quantities, from the frontier to the cities in the east. Likewise, finished products such as tables and chairs made by urban artisans could easily be shipped to villages and forts on the frontier. These examples show various ways the Erie Canal helped knit together this new and sprawling nation and ushered in a new age of trade and travel.

The Assignment

With the help of an atlas, draw a map of New York State. Include New York City, the Hudson River, Albany, the Erie Canal, Buffalo and Lake Erie. Along the Canal, draw signs that say, "No Swimmers, Fast Lane," "4 M.P.H.," "5 Cents per Mile," "Caution," "Low Bridge," and "Hold On! Lock Ahead." Show a mule pulling one of the boats while thinking, "Four miles an hour! I need more hay!"

Possible Title

Getting Connected

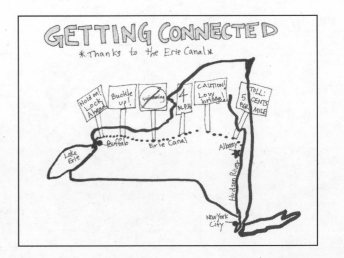

Read ★ Draw ★ Remember American History Activities

The War of 1812

The History

*I*n 1812, President Madison declared war against Great Britain. Madison was angry with the British for two reasons. First, they were capturing American trading ships, kidnapping American sailors, and forcing them to work in the British Navy. Second, the British were refusing to leave their forts on America's frontier. This conflict was called The War of 1812, even though fighting went on until 1815. The most devastating blow came when the British marched into Washington and burned the Capitol Building and the White House. Then they set their sights on Baltimore.

Baltimore Harbor was guarded by star-shaped Fort McHenry. Earlier in the war, Mary Pickersgill, a Baltimore flag maker, had sewn a huge American flag to fly over the fort. It was 42 feet by 30 feet and had 15 stripes and 15 stars.

When the British sailed into the harbor, they were met by a boat waving the white flag of truce. On this boat was Francis Scott Key, a Washington lawyer who'd been sent to negotiate a prisoner exchange. Key got an American doctor released, but their truce ship was not allowed to return until the fighting was over.

All night long, the British pounded Fort McHenry with canon balls. The attack continued the next day and through a second night. At dawn the following morning, Key was thrilled to see the American flag still flying over the battered fort, and he put some words on paper. His poem was published in Baltimore. It was called, "The Defense of Fort McHenry." Soon people were singing Key's words, and the song was given a new title: "The Star-Spangled Banner."

The Assignment

Look up the meaning of the words *ramparts* and *perilous*. And realize that *O'er* is a way of saying *over*. Then read the first verse of "The Star-Spangled Banner."

> *Oh! say can you see, by the dawn's early light,*
> *What so proudly we hailed at the twilight's last gleaming?*
> *Whose broad stripes and bright stars, through the perilous fight,*
> *O'er the ramparts we watched were so gallantly streaming.*
> *And the rockets' red glare, the bombs bursting in air,*
> *Gave proof through the night that our flag was still there.*
> *Oh! say, does that star-spangled banner yet wave*
> *O'er the land of the free and the home of the brave?*

Draw the scene of the bombs bursting over Fort McHenry, the flag flying, and the ships in the harbor. Write phrases from the song at appropriate places to label your drawing.

Possible Title

The Creation of the U.S. National Anthem

Read ★ Draw ★ Remember American History Activities

The Missouri Compromise

The History

By 1819, the United States consisted of 11 free states and 11 slave states. That meant that in the debate over slavery each side had 22 Senators in the United States Senate, and, as a result, no laws could be passed that hurt one side or the other. The question then arose of how to admit another state into the union without tipping the balance. The answer was the Missouri Compromise of 1820. Under that law, Missouri entered the union as a slave state, Maine entered as a free state, and the balance of power didn't change.

The Assignment

Think of how you might illustrate a balance between two sides. You might choose to draw a scale, a seesaw, or the long pole of a tightrope walker. Whatever you select, find a way to use the names of the states involved. For example, if you choose a scale, you might put 12 blocks on one side, label them "Slave States," and then write these abbreviations on them: "AL," "DE," "GA," "KY," "LA," "MD," "MS," "NC," "SC," "TN," and "VA." Add "MO" to the top. Label the other side "Free States" and write these abbreviations on the blocks: "CT," "IL," "IN," "MA," "NH," "NJ," "NY," "OH," "PA," "RI," and "VT." Add "ME" to the top of the blocks on this side.

Possible Title

The Missouri Compromise

Read ★ Draw ★ Remember American History Activities

Trails West

The History

B eginning in the 1820s, great numbers of Americans began heading to the far west. Whether it was for freedom, adventure, opportunity, or profit, wagon trains began making the 800-mile trip from Franklin, Missouri, to Santa Fe, New Mexico. Josiah Gregg went west with 100 wagons in 1831, and he later wrote, "The arrival [in Santa Fe] produced a great deal of bustle and excitement among the natives. 'Los Americanos!'—'Los carros!'—'La entrada de la caravana!' were to be heard in every direction; and crowds of women and boys flocked around to see the newcomers."

Other pioneers attempted the treacherous, 2,000-mile journey from Independence, Missouri, to the west coast. Despite such obstacles as snow capped mountain ranges and blistering deserts, 3,000 people traveled west on the Oregon and California Trails in 1845. A year later, a group of 87 people—men, women, and children—left Illinois and headed west. This was the infamous Donner Party. A blinding snowstorm would eventually trap them in the Sierras and many would perish.

One group of westward settlers did not go willingly. These were the Cherokee Indians who lived in Georgia and who were ordered off their beloved land when Congress passed the Indian Removal Act of 1830. The Cherokee fought this law, and their case went all the way to the Supreme Court. The Court agreed with the Cherokee, but, incredibly, President Andrew Jackson ignored the Court's decision. He sent soldiers to force the Cherokee out of Georgia. They walked to Oklahoma on what is called the "Trail of Tears."

The Assignment

Divide your paper into thirds. In the first third, draw a wagon heading west on the Santa Fe Trail. Behind the wagon, draw a map and the route from Missouri to New Mexico. On the side of the wagon, draw a happy face. On the second third, draw a wagon and a map of the Oregon Trail. Put a happy face on the side of this wagon. In the third section, draw a wagon and a map of the Trail of Tears. Put a sad face on the side of the wagon.

Possible Title

Triumph and Tragedy

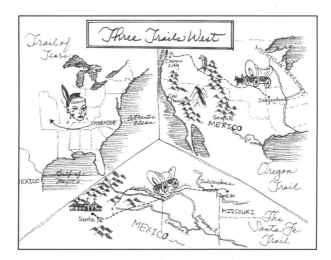

The Lowell Cotton Mills

The History

The first cotton mills in Lowell, Massachusetts, were built in 1823. Next to the mills were dormitories to house an unusual group of workers. These were the teenage girls who had left their family farms in Maine, New Hampshire, and Vermont and journeyed to Lowell to work in the mills for $2 a week. By tending the looms and the spindles, and by working 13 hours a day, these smart and nimble-fingered girls were able to earn five times more than a schoolteacher did. Many of the mill girls sent money home to pay the mortgage on the family farm or to put a brother through Harvard. The mill owners used this skilled and literate labor force to produce tremendous amounts of cloth, which was exported all over the world. The mill owners got rich and built more mills. By 1834, there were almost 5,000 girls working in the Lowell cotton mills. This was the beginning of the industrial revolution in America.

The Assignment

Draw a mill girl wearing a long dress, an apron, and a bonnet and lifting a barbell over her head. Where the weights normally are, draw two circles. Inside one of the circles, write "Wealthy Mill Owners" and inside the other write "Happy Investors." Another approach would be to draw three mill girls standing on the bottom of a human pyramid. Draw and label two "Stockholders" standing on their shoulders and the "Mill Owner" (in his top hat) on top.

Possible Title

America's New Labor Force

The Monroe Doctrine

The History

By 1820, the once mighty nation of Spain had seen its wealth diminish and its power wane. As a result it lost control of many of its colonies in the Americas. Other, stronger European nations were eager to move in and colonize these lands. President James Monroe didn't want any more European neighbors who might inhibit American growth. So, in 1821, he bought Florida from Spain for $5 million. Then, in December 1823, he made a speech to Congress, but the speech was really directed at European nations. He said that from that day forward, the United States would not allow any more European colonies in North America, South America, and Central America. In return, he said that the United States would stay out of European affairs. This stay-out-of-my-backyard policy became known as the "Monroe Doctrine."

The Assignment

Think of food that might be vulnerable to an insect attack. You might put a pie on a windowsill. Label the pie "The Americas." Draw some flies heading for the pie and label the flies "European Nations." Draw a hand holding a fly swatter. Label the hand "President Monroe" and label the fly swatter "The Monroe Doctrine."

Possible Title

Monroe says, "No."

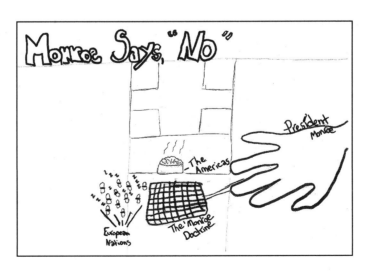

The Mexican-American War

The History

In 1846, President James Polk declared war on Mexico. The war, called the Mexican-American War, was fought for land. Some American slave owners wanted the army to take all of Mexico so cotton plantations could be established south of the Rio Grande River. But other Americans did not support this war. Writer Henry David Thoreau, who wrote a famous book called *Walden*, refused to pay taxes because he didn't want that money used to support this war. He was thrown in jail. Frederick Douglass, the abolitionist, wrote, "Those who have been loudly in favor of the war have succeeded in robbing Mexico of her territory. We are not the people to rejoice; we ought rather blush and hang our heads for shame." And a 38-year-old Congressman named Abraham Lincoln said, "Allow the president to invade a neighboring nation whenever he may choose to and you allow him to make war at pleasure." But Polk had enough supporters and plenty of talented generals (including Robert E. Lee and Ulysses S. Grant), and soon American soldiers were fighting in Mexico City.

When the war ended, with the signing of a treaty in 1848, it was decided that the border between Mexico and Texas would be the Rio Grande river. But there was something else in this treaty—called the Treaty of Guadalupe Hidalgo—that proved of greater significance. Mexico sold California and New Mexico to the United States for $15,000,000. And, it so happened, that earlier that year a man working at Sutter's Mill in northern California had come across something shiny and golden.

The Assignment

In the parking lot of a supermarket, draw a man putting a shopping bag into the back of a car. Label the car "United States—1848." Label the man "President Polk." Label the shopping bag "California." Draw a glittering rock sticking out of the shopping bag.

Possible Title

The Treaty of Guadalupe Hidalgo

The Immigrant Experience

The History

Since 1492, America has been a land of immigrants. In 1630, you could already hear 18 different languages being spoken in the city of New Amsterdam. From 1820 to 1930, the United States received about 60 percent of the world's immigrants. There were many factors that drove people to leave their homelands, including famine, religious persecution, lack of jobs, a population explosion in Europe, and improved transportation. What brought them to America was the promise of religious freedom, the opportunity to own land, and the need for workers in America's factories and on the railroads.

The Assignment

Think of how you might illustrate the immigrant experience. One way would be to draw a squirrel jumping from a sad-looking tree to another strong, leafy one. Or you could show a man jumping off a diving board into a pool. Include the reasons (mentioned above) why a person might leave his old country and embark on a new life.

Possible Title

America the Beautiful

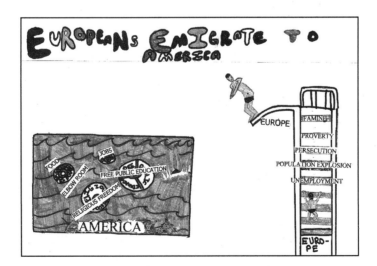

Differences Lead to the Civil War

The History

The Civil War (1860–1865) was a battle between the southern slave states (also called the Confederate States) and the northern free states. But it was also a battle between two different economic systems. The southern economy was based on agriculture. Huge fortunes had been made by men whose slaves picked the cotton and indigo and harvested the rice and tobacco. The northern states, on the other hand, had more industry. In fact, in 1861, the North had 98 percent of the factories in America. Ninety-seven percent of the firearms produced in America were made in the North. The South had only 9,000 miles of railroad tracks compared with 21,000 in the North. This industrial strength would help power the North to victory over the South.

The Assignment

Think of how you might illustrate a southern agrarian (or farm) society taking on the northern industrial society. You might try a bull and a matador or a farmer facing down a locomotive. Or you might want to draw the belching smoke from a factory blanketing the cotton fields. Label the two antagonists "Southern Farming Economy" and "Northern Industrial Economy."

Possible Title

The Civil War—Tradition Versus Innovation

The Emancipation Proclamation

The History

On August 22, 1862, in the middle of the Civil War, President Abraham Lincoln wrote a letter to a newspaper editor named Horace Greeley. He said, "If I could save the union without freeing any slave, I would do it; and if I could save it by freeing all the slaves, I would do it; and if I could do it by freeing some and leaving others alone, I would also do that." Lincoln chose the third option. On January 1, 1863, Lincoln issued the Emancipation Proclamation which freed only those slaves who lived in states that were still in rebellion against the United States. Lincoln called the Proclamation "an act of justice, warranted by the Constitution and by military necessity." On the day he signed it, he said, "I never, in my life, felt more certain that I was doing right, than I do in signing this paper." Slaves who lived in other states would eventually be freed by future legislation or by the 13th Amendment to the Constitution which was ratified in 1865.

The Assignment

Think of how you might illustrate an end to slavery. One way might be to show a sledgehammer coming down and breaking an iron chain or pulverizing a boulder. You might also show a big fist punching through a door. Label the chain, boulder, or door "Slavery."

Possible Title

The Emancipation Proclamation—1/1/1863

The Battle of Gettysburg

The History

In late June 1863, after his victory at the battle of Chancellorsville, Confederate General Robert E. Lee decided to invade the North. His plan was to march his army into Pennsylvania and then turn southeast and attack Washington, D.C. He was confident of victory. In his pocket he had papers of surrender that he was sure President Lincoln would soon be signing. In the Pennsylvania town of Gettysburg, the Union forces met Lee's Army of Northern Virginia. It would prove to be a turning point of the Civil War. After three days of fierce fighting, almost 50,000 men were killed, wounded, or missing. Lee withdrew on July 4th and his weary army headed back to Virginia. Neither Lee nor his troops would ever recover from their loss at Gettysburg.

The Assignment

Think of an animal grazing in a peaceful, grassy setting. Label the animal "Army of Northern Virginia." Label the grass "Southern Victories." Draw a lion or some other predator of the grazing animal lurking in the tall grass. Label this animal "Gettysburg."

Possible Title

The Battle of Gettysburg, July 1–3, 1863

The Underground Railroad

The History

The Underground Railroad was neither underground nor a railroad. It was a metaphor that first appeared in the early 1840s, and it described an escape route for southern slaves. That route included safe houses (called "stations") where runaway slaves (called "passengers") were helped by abolitionists and free blacks (called "conductors"). On the most dangerous sections of their routes, primarily in the deep South, the slaves were usually on their own. If and when they made it to Cincinnati, Ohio, Philadelphia, Pennsylvania, or Wilmington, Delaware, the "conductors" would hide them, feed them, and guide them. Harriett Tubman was one of these "conductors." Between 1840 and 1860, the Underground Railroad helped approximately 20,000 slaves escape to freedom in the northern states or Canada.

The Assignment

Think of a way to bridge a gap. Perhaps it's a rock in the middle of a stream that allows a frog to hop from one side of the stream (the South) to the other side (Canada). Label the rock "Underground Railroad." Label the frog "Escaped Slave."

Possible Title

Escape to Freedom on the Underground Railroad

Notes